This novel consists of a literature review I wrote while getting my Masters of Arts in Management Degree at Doane University graduating with a 3.998 GPA in December 2011.

LEONARD G CERNIK
5/18/09

UNANIMOUS ANONYMOUS V -TELEPATHY-ESP- REALITY?

2

UNANIMOUS ANONYMOUS V -TELEPATHY-ESP- REALITY?

How real is Telepathy and ESP?

Review of Literature

Leonard G Cernik

Doane University

Masters of Arts in Management

MAM program

Foundations of Research BUS

May 18, 2009

How real is Telepathy and ESP?

Introduction

The world is searching to find out if telepathy and ESP (Extra Sensory Perception) is real. Based upon the amount of research that has been conducted in this area of interest there is a good possibility telepathy is a real phenomena. Additional research in other similar areas of study indicated differing degrees of confirmation of telepathy and ESP. Some studies showed indications that telepathy and ESP is more than mere chance. Other studies indicate that based on statistical probability, the probability of telepathy and ESP's existence

was equal to that of chance.

Brown and Sheldrake (2001)

surveyed two hundred people. The

researchers found that three quarters

(seventy-eight percent) of the people

surveyed said that they telephoned someone

who said they were just thinking about

telephoning them. Besides this response to

telephone calls, forty-five per cent of those

surveyed said they experienced other

situations that seemed to involve telepathy.

A quarter of these people (twenty-two

percent) said that their seemingly telepathic

experiences happen often. These surveys

were conducted in California and indicated

there is a good percentage of chance that telepathy and ESP does exist. If these surveys are reliable, they provide evidence to support the reality of telepathy and ESP.

Sheldrake and Smart (2003) conducted more experiments that indicated a high percentage of chance that telepathy and ESP may occur. They conducted two hundred seventy-one experiments, all videotaped to eliminate the possibility of cheating. Participants in telephony videotaped experiments gave significant, repeatable results. When callers were known, there was a sixty-one percent success rate in predicting the caller and a forty-one percent success rate in prediction among unfamiliar callers. The experiments'

results are additional evidence to support the

reality of telepathy and ESP. These

experiments occurred in the every day

environment of anticipation and prediction

of contacts by phone calling. Distance

between telephone callers was not a factor

and more than mere chance.

Sheldrake and Smart in the press

(July 2003), described the results of five

hundred seventy trials involving sixty-three

participants. Findings showed that the

average success rate was forty percent,

which is hugely significant statistically.

Distance between callers was not a factor in

that during these trials the callers were miles

apart, and in some cases thousands of miles

apart. The results would imply that the

participants' above-chance success rate was

a result of telepathy from the callers.

Smith (2005) discusses Sheldrake's

theory. . Sheldrake believes such

phenomena are examples of 'seventh sense'.

Sheldrake used the term 'seventh sense'

since the more traditional 'sixth sense' is

now more commonly used in the scientific

community to refer to certain sensory

activity found in the animal kingdom but not

among humans. There has also been

research indicating that owners and their

pets have telepathic connections in cases

where the pet knows when the owner is

coming home, even at large distances

between the owner and pet. Sheldrake has

said that in research by Sir Rudolph Peters, a

mentally retarded child sensed things

through his mother, even when miles apart.

The researcher theorized that this may be

due to the intensity of the bond between

mother and child. This bond may have

developed because-it was necessary for the

child's survival.

This literature review will focus on

areas confirming or contradicting that

telepathy and ESP are real phenomena. In

the end, it will present conclusions on

information about how real is telepathy and

ESP. This review will discuss the following

themes: the reality of telepathy, the relationship to ESP, the Psi phenomena, brain wave patterns that can be measured and read with sensors and MRI, and Ganzfeld experiments, which are experiments that measure ESP among test subjects.

Reality of Telepathy

Brown and Sheldrake (2001) conducted a survey in California on the anticipation of telephone calls. Two hundred random people were surveyed in Santa Cruz County, California. Data was collected by means of telephone surveys. Two hundred people participated. (Seventy-eight men and one hundred twenty-two women) Seventy-eight percent telephoned someone who said

they were thinking about them.   In the

survey forty-seven percent, also new who

was calling them before answering the

phone. Sixty-eight percent said they had

thought of someone who later telephoned

that day. Some of these could have chance

experiences, and others might have

depended on telepathy. Two previous

surveys in London and Greater Manchester

England indicate this experience happens

quite frequently. The surveys are just

another means of evaluating Telepathy.

Sheldrake and Smart (2003)

videotaped experiments on telephone

telepathy. Participants were videotaped

during experimental period using four

potential callers with one selected randomly.

Two hundred seventy-one trials were

conducted. The actual experiment used

telephone anticipation instead of just survey.

Random chance would indicate twenty five

percent correct responses. The study of two

hundred seventy-one total trials indicated

forty-five percent correct guesses. With

familiar callers, there was a sixty-one

percent success rate. Video taping trials

reduced chance of cheating, if not making it

virtually impossible.

There was a research report rebuttal

written to the Editor (2003) of the

journal that commented on Rupert

Sheldrake's and Pam Smart's paper,

"Videotaped experiments on telephone

telepathy" The letter to the editor stated

that data presented from experiments on

telephone telepathy may be in error. In

one of the specific analyses Sheldrake

reported a significantly different hit rate

dependent on whether the subjects were

called by familiar or unfamiliar callers.

The differences are reported in report to

be "very significant statistically" and

according to Sheldrake the significant

difference "supports an interpretation in

terms of telepathy". The letter to the

editor stated that they disagreed with the

analysis and the conclusion. They

claimed that Sheldrake's conclusion

was based on a statistically

unsatisfactory procedure. The letter to

the editor did comment that their

critique applied only to the comparison

of familiar and unfamiliar callers. The

overall hit rate of the entire experiment

remains untouched by their reanalysis.

Sheldrake and Smart (July 2003)

described the results of five hundred seventy

trials involving sixty-three participants. The

participants were recruited through

advertisements in a part time work section

of newspapers or through a recruitment web

site.   These trials were a confirmation test

for earlier studies. The significance is that

these trials further documented the reality of telepathy. The findings were reported in correct determination of the random phone caller chosen between four potential callers. The overall success rate in caller determination was forty percent. This was hugely significant since it was above the twenty-five percent success rate expected based upon chance or random guessing. The emotional closeness of callers seemed to be more important than the physical proximity.

Smith (2005) wrote an article on telepathy research. Smith commented that far from being a cranky relic of a pre-Enlightenment dark age, the belief in telepathy would seem to be confirmed by contemporary science. Smith further

commented in that telepathy might even

help secure the planet's survival. Smith puts

together a good summary on telepathic

research and insights into Sheldrake's work

and Sheldrake's professor at Cambridge.

This article lists Sheldrake's web site

www.sheldrake.org. This general

presentation on topics related to the reality

of telepathy was a good overview, providing

research direction in finding proof for the

reality of telepathy.

Vassy (2004) conducted a study of

telepathy by classical conditioning.

Experiments were conducted detecting

telepathy by classical conditioning using a

mild electric shock. The stimulus was a

telepathic message and the unconditional

response was the sudden rise in skin

conductance. Fifty sessions of ten electric

shocks were conducted, using conditioning

assuming telepathy involves yet unidentified

physiological process in the brain. Earlier

studies were conducted in 1997 and 1978.

There were significantly positive results in

fifty runs. **A r**eplication study showed that

the first experiment could not be replicated,

thus raising questions about the study

Skeptic (2001) magazine showed

results of a survey conducted on June 8,

2001 by the Gallup news service poll

showing paranormal beliefs are on the rise.

UNANIMOUS ANONYMOUS V -TELEPATHY-ESP-REALITY?

One thousand twelve adults eighteen years old or older were surveyed, conducted May 10-14, 2001 with a ninety-five percent confidence level. Eighteen to twenty-nine year olds are more likely to believe in telepathy and clairvoyance. People age thirty and older had different beliefs. Religious beliefs were a factor. Survey results showed that in telepathy thirty-six percent believed, twenty-six percent were not sure, and thirty-five percent don't believe. In two surveys on the belief in telepathy results showed that thirty-six percent believed in 2001, in a survey in 1990 thirty-six percent, these results show there was a zero percent change in between the two studies. Besides telepathy, other paranormal beliefs were

studied, but belief in telepathy had not

changed over time.

Sheldrake and Smart (2005)

investigated possible telepathic

communication in connection with e-mails.

Trials were conducted with four potential e-

mailers, one of whom was selected at

random by the experimenter. One minute

before a prearranged time at which the e-

mail was to be sent, the participant guessed

who would send it. Fifty participants

(twenty-nine women and twenty-one men)

were recruited through an employment web

site. Five hundred fifty-two trials were

conducted. The results of two hundred

thirty-five guesses (forty-three percent) were

hits. This is significantly above the chance

expectation of Twenty-five percent. Further

tests with five participants (four women, one

man, and ages sixteen to twenty-nine) were

videotaped continuously. On the filmed

trials, the sixty-four hits of one hundred

thirty-seven trials or forty-seven percent

were significantly above chance that

expected by chance

Sheldrake, Godwin, and Rockell

(2004) carried out experiments in an attempt

to replicate the telephone telepathy

phenomenon for a television show called

"Are You Telepathic?" made by *20/20*

Productions and broadcast in the UK on

UNANIMOUS ANONYMOUS V -TELEPATHY-ESP- REALITY?

Channel Five Television on June 19, 2003.

The participant and her four callers were

Sisters, who had for years worked together

in a girl band, the Nolan Sisters, popular in

the UK in the 1980s. In most of the trials,

the callers were in different locations from

each other and were not filmed... However

in one previous experiment, all four callers

were in the same location, and the callers as

well as the participant were filmed

continuously. The test, carried out in

Wakefield, Yorkshire, placed the participant

one point five km away from the four

callers. One of the sisters guessed correctly

in eight out of seventeen trials (forty-seven

percent); Sheldrake concludes that the

results support the hypothesis of telepathic

communication. Of course, further

replications will be needed, and in future

tests it would be desirable to rule out the

possibility of cheating using mobile phones.

Wassner (2005) presented five

stories about twins that have similar

thoughts giving some proof to the reality of

telepathy. The article stated that not all

identical twins share a connection. This

paper presents an example of five stories in

which twins seem to be connected mentally

in various ways. This is a general

presentation of stories about identical twins

providing examples where twins seem to

have a connection that cannot be explained

by today's societies view of what would be

classed as a normal relationship.

Sheldrake (2006) used a telephone

survey method to question nursing mothers

about their reactions to when their baby

needed them. Some nursing mothers

claimed that when they are away from their

baby they often knew when their baby

needed them because their milk lets down.

Some mothers were convinced that this

response is telepathic. Sheldrake, in order to

find out more about this phenomenon,

surveyed one hundred mothers who had

recently had babies and asked a series of

questions about their experiences when

breastfeeding. Sixty-two percent had

experienced milk let-down when away from their babies. Sixteen percent had noticed that this seemed to coincide with their baby needing them. Most of these women had breastfed their babies for more than six months. In addition, three women said they had felt there was something wrong with their baby when they were away from home, and found that it was indeed in distress because of a fall or other accident. Five women commented that they often woke up shortly before their baby needed them in the night. These surveys used babies and mothers in another way of evaluating telepathy. Apart from the phenomenon of milk let-down, in question ten of all mothers in this survey were asked "While you were away from your baby, have you ever had a strong sense that your baby needs you, other than through your milk letting down?" Thirty-one out of one hundred answered yes to this question. Most of these women said in response to a previous question that this may be a matter of general anxiety or intuition. Several women commented that their anxiety was more related to their own worries than to their baby's needs. However, three women reported that they had felt something was wrong with their baby and either telephoned home or went to the baby and found that it was in distress because of a fall or other accident. Five women commented that they often woke up shortly before the baby needed them in the night.

Sheldrake (2005) presented various views based upon different people staring at other people or sensing that they were being stared at. Sheldrake presented different theories of how non-visual staring can mentally be detected. Sheldrake theorized that features of the perceptual fields may have implications for the understanding of morphic fields. The morphic fields may be related to patterns of activity in the electromagnetic fields of the brain but may be also separable from other electromagnetic fields. The brain can project virtual images in three dimensions with the basis of these patterns being electromag-

netic activity. The morphic fields may

interact with patterns of electromagnetic

activity not only through the eyes but

elsewhere in the in the brain. This

electromagnetic activity in an individual

brain may be picked up by other people.

Sheldrake and Smart (2000)

conducted video taped experiments and

observations on one dog and one owner.

They video taped the dog at a window

during owners absence and when the owner

was returning home. Various observations

of the dogs' behavior were conducted in

controlled environment and different

environments.

UNANIMOUS ANONYMOUS V -TELEPATHY-ESP-REALITY?

These experiments were unique because the tests involved an animal. This presents the possibility that animals and not only humans may have telepathic or ESP abilities.

The test dog was far more at the window waiting when owner was on her way home than when she was not on her way home.

The results were displayed in tables and graphs. Replication experiment showed similar results. The suggestion was made that dog was detecting owners' intention to come home. The testing removed the chance that anticipation of the owners return was based on time of day or consistent return times.

Sheldrake and Morgan (2003)

conducted trials with one parrot and one

owner. One hundred forty-seven, two

minute trials, using video tape equipment in

the experiment with parrot and owner placed

in different rooms. The owner would open

up an envelope with a word that the parrot

knew how to say. Seventy one trials showed

positive results of the parrot saying the word

corresponding to the picture that the owner

looked at in the other room. . Findings were

consistent with the hypothesis that the parrot

was responding telepathically to owner's

mental activity. This study was unique in

that it used a parrot in the experiments.

UNANIMOUS ANONYMOUS V -TELEPATHY-ESP-REALITY?

Sheldrake (2000) noted the most common kinds of seemingly telepathic responses are the anticipation by dogs and cats of their owners coming home. The animals may also anticipate the owner's intention of going away. Also they may anticipate the owner getting ready to feed them. Sheldrake believes that there is much potential for further research on animal telepathy. Sheldrake theorizes that if domestic animals are telepathic with their human owners, then there is a possibility that the animals are telepathic with each other. This may play an important part in the wild. The newsletter discourse sheds some light on telepathy and ESP in the animal world theorizing that telepathy from people

to animals usually occurs only when there

are close emotional bonds. Emotional bonds

may also be an important factor in human

telepathy.

Sheldrake, Lawlor, and Turney

conducted a telephone survey on perceptive

pets. The survey was conducted in London

by telephone, with the intent to find out how

many pet owners had observed seemingly

telepathic abilities in their pets. Fifty-two

percent of dog owners claimed that their

animals knew in advance when a member of

the household was on the way home,

compared with twenty-four percent of cat

owners. Of the animals that reacted.

Twenty-one percent of dogs and nineteen

percent of cats were said to do so more than

ten minutes before the persons return.

Seventy-three percent of dog owners and

fifty-two percent of cat owners said their

pets knew when the owners were going out

before they showed any signs of doing so.

Forty-three percent of dog owners and forty-

one percent of cat owners said their pets

responded to their thoughts or silent com-

mands; and fifty-seven percent of dog

owners and thirty-seven percent of cat

owners said their pets were sometimes

telepathic with them. Forty-six percent of

people with pets now and thirty-seven

percent of people without pets now said that

they had known pets in the past that were

telepathic. Thirty nine percent of those with

pets now and thirty-eight percent of those

currently without pets said they themselves

had had psychic experiences. But

significantly fewer of those who had never

kept pets had had psychic experiences

themselves. The results of this survey are

compared with two similar surveys in North-

West England and in California. The general

pattern was remarkably similar in these three

very different locations and shows that

seemingly telepathic abilities in pets are

common. In all locations dogs were more

responsive than cats to their owners'

thoughts and intentions. Results based on

this survey are subject to error since it

involves the perceptions of the pet owners

without thorough experimental trials to

prove claims.

Thomas and Fletcher (2003)

conducted test on the mind reading accuracy

in intimate relationships. The study tested

for the moderating effects of the judge,

target, and relationship on mind-reading

accuracy during intimate problem-solving

interactions. The study used a video-review

procedure, multiple perceivers judged

multiple targets at different levels of

acquaintanceship (dating partners vs. friends

vs. strangers). The study also investigated

the role of three relationship-level predictors

of mind-reading accuracy (for dating

couples and friends): relationship

satisfaction, closeness, and prior disclosure

about the problems discussed."

Their conclusions were that by

systematically examining the relationship

between the perceiver and the target, the

study was able to disentangle the

contributions made by the relationship, the

target, and the judge in terms of mind-

reading accuracy. It was found that all three

moderators played a role. It was mentioned

that the nature of the relationship between

the judge and the target exerted the most

profound effects. This moderated the

influence of the target and the judge in both expected and unexpected ways.

This was a unique study in that it evaluated intimate relationships in a documented study. An important aspect of this study was the finding that mind-reading accuracy does not reach a plateau at a certain level of friendship, but goes up a notch in the context of intimate romantic relationships. The study does demonstrate acquaintanceship effects in both mind reading and personality domains.

DeGraaf and Houtkooper (2004) evaluated emotional awareness with tests on individuals who have experienced past emotional trauma. Twelve subjects were asked to guess the top down sequence of

symbols in an open deck of one hundred

Zener Cards. Four cases were studied. The

researchers assumption in of this

experiment was that a strong

unconscious wish or "intentionality" to

express the emotions connected with

certain pictures could cause relatively

more correspondences with Zener cards

(ZTs)--or, in fact, their simulations--at

certain "sensitive spots. The Zener

targets were located at the twelve

"sensitive spots," i.e., the exact locations

of the twelve pictures. Using the twelve

pictures also showed that subjects with

the higher trauma scores were able to

pick the twelve pictures out and the

pictures attracted considerably more

displacements of all types than pictures

which the subject had left aside in the

initial review. The study suggested that

these findings could be a result of

conscious choice between the pictures

mentioned and pictures not mentioned.

This may have mirrored the emotional

significance that the subjects had also

unconsciously bestowed to twelve

pictures, which may. This could explain

the general lack of significant

correlations between trauma scores and

displacement types for pictures not

mentioned. These tests were a further

evaluation in a different way of relating

telepathy to emotion.

Murray, Howard, Wilde, Fez, and

Simmonds-Moore (2007) tested for

telepathy using an immersive virtual

environment. They say there are a number

of advantages over Ganzfeld work using

static or dynamic stimuli or immersive

virtual environment. Two hundred males,

one hundred twelve females, were tested in

pairs at The University of Manchester.

The experimenters used computer

technology to set up an immersive virtual

reality environment. This was a new type of

computerized testing which they felt was

superior to the Ganzfeld standard

computerized test procedures. The study did

not find results to support the Psi hypothesis.

The results could be used to argue for the

nonexistence of Psi. The Ganzfeld test lasts

for two hours and these tests lasted seven

minutes. That difference could be criticism

for using too short of a time. This too short

of test time and test procedures may have

resulted in poor results.

Moss and Gengerelli (1967)

conducted a controlled experiment on

telepathy and emotional stimuli. The study

was an attempt to simulate in some small

measure the strong affects which appear to

accompany spontaneous telepathic events.

The test used stimuli and after each stimulus

episode, the participant spoke their

reactions, which were recorded verbatim.

After a suitable delay between tests, a

second emotional episode was presented.

The study conducted in a controlled

laboratory indicates that something like

telepathy occurs between two people,

isolated from each other, when the

Transmitter is emotionally aroused and the

Receiver is lying down, relaxed. The results

showed that seven out of twelve professional

psychologists and psychiatrists matched the

protocols of fifty experimental T-R teams

which is significantly better than that of

chance expectation However it was found

that under two controlled conditions

involving thirteen and ten T-R teams,

respectively, only one of the same twelve

judges matched in these tests which is better

than chance.

This study was included because it

was one of the forerunners to current studies

on telepathy and emotion. It however

showed results that indicated further study

was necessary because at that time telepathy

was considered abnormal phenomena that

most researchers dismissed as coincidence.

Relationship to ESP

Tressold and Prete (2007) studied

ESP with subjects under hypnosis. Twelve

volunteers (seven males and five females)

who attend authors' center were tested. Two

types of hypnotic induction were used.

Those tested used simple gambling tasks.

The author's use of hypnosis to evaluate

ESP was compared to other hypnosis

studies. The results used standard statistical

comparisons. Thirty-three percent of correct

hits were recorded in the first session.

Twenty-four percent correct hits were

recorded in the second session. The results

indicated that people in a hypnotic state may

be more conducive to psi phenomena. The

conclusion was that further study is needed.

Colwell, Schroder, and Sladen

(2000) stated that there was evidence to

suggest that individuals not only believe in

their ability to detect an unseen gaze, but

may actually be able to do so. Twelve

volunteers were recruited on the basis of

their belief in ESP. The volunteers were

placed in closed rooms with one way

mirrors. The responses were recorded on a

computer. The median age was twenty-four

with seven men and five women tested who

where in the nineteen to forty-nine year old

age range. This test was significant because

selection of the volunteers were based on

their belief in ESP. The test results showed

little support for the staring detection effect

on non feed back trials. In feedback trials

the response bias was present. The two

experiments conducted showed no proof that

staring could be detected. The authors cited

Sheldrake (1994) in this research paper.

Sheldrake suggested that the effect is

difficult to obtain in artificial conditions,

presumably as found in this research study.

Wiseman and Greening (2002)

conducted a mass participation experiment

where participants were asked to complete

an ESP task that involved them guessing the

outcome of four random electronic coin

tosses. All data was stored on computers.

The researchers aimed to help resolve ESP

debate by devising a novel procedure for

carrying out a large scale force choice ESP

Experiment. Mind machine consisted of

computer based video clips related to coin

tosses. The final database contained twenty

seven thousand eight hundred fifty-six

participants, Two hundred fifty thousand

data points with one hundred thirty-nine

thousand forty three data points from five

question tests and one hundred ten thousand

nine hundred fifty-nine data points from

ESP trials. The Over all outcome showed

results did not differ from that of chance and

all of the internal analyses were non-

significant. The mind machine took place in

noisy public spaces and not in quiet

laboratory surroundings. The study may

have failed because forced-choice ESP may

not exist.

Owens and Pitman (2004) conducted

a study with the aim to manipulate

expectations or attitudes before and during a test of ESP. Thirty one student volunteers at University of Glamorgan were used in tests consisting of six males and twenty five females. They were randomly assigned to four conditions. Participants ages were between eighteen and forty seven with mean of twenty five. Participants were tested individually by one experimenter. Some were given a placebo stating that it enhanced ESP abilities and tested without a placebo. The Experiment used the Australian Sheep-goat scale, a computerized test. Participants asked how they were going to test for ESP before given out a possible Twenty-five correct guesses selected from five possible

targets.

Experiment expected to test two

connected hypotheses. First that ESP

performance would be positive affected by

the manipulation expectance prior and

during test and second that this result would

be most evident with the indecisive group

who did not believe in ESP.

Two Experiments were conducted

with both experiments showing that ESP

Performance was highest with Placebo or

high false expectations. There was a

possible relationship to the self-efficacy

perspective which increased expectance to

the degree of participant success in scoring

high in ESP.

Psi Phenomena

Psi denotes anomalous processes of

information or energy transfer. These

processes may be telepathy or other forms of

extrasensory perception. The term is used in

relation to all currently unexplained

phenomena in physical or biological

mechanisms.

Bem and Honorton (retrieved 2009)

Does psi exist? According to survey

conducted by researchers, most academic

psychologist does not think so. One

thousand one hundred college professors in

the United States surveyed found that fifty-five percent of the natural scientists, sixty-

six percent of social scientists and seventy-

seven percent of academics in the arts,

humanities, and education believe that ESP

is either an established fact or a likely

possibility. A comparable to psychologist

was that only thirty-four percent thought it

was possible. An equal number of

psychologists believe that ESP is

impossibility, a view expressed by only two

percent of all other respondents. The study

goes on to list various aspects of areas of psi

research.

Alexander and Broughton (2001)

developed an automated testing system

using equipment called Autoganzfeld H

which uses the same hardware and software

as that used to control Ganzfeld experiments

as that used to accumulate the raw data files

by Psychophysical Research Laboratories

that closed in 1989. Right brain hemisphere

dominance was measured by a procedure

called CLB. The results were then related to

the Ganzfeld procedure. The scoring was

related to the direct hit method. Participant

scoring right hemisphere dominance as

measured by CLB scored significantly more

direct hits in Autoganzfeld than those with

left cerebral hemisphere dominance. There

was no conclusive evidence of brain and psi

phenomena. However, the part of the brain

that has potential for further Psi phenomena

was identified which makes this study

significant.

Carpenter (2008) summarizes

research that has been directed toward the

Psi phenomena. Carpenter presents

information and provides an overview of Psi

theory, summary of researchers conducting

test, and general findings and hypothesis.

There are three pages of references listed in

back of research article. This paper is

important because it summarizes the

theories and beliefs on ESP and Psi, plus

some of the research that has been

conducted to date. It better helps understand

what has been done.

The psi model asserts

that the earliest source of

potential information comes

from our non local

engagement with reality. This

preconscious process happens

very quickly when our

conscious experience flows

along. Psi is assumed to be

quite a normal process, which

can quickly be deployed and

quickly abandoned. Psi is

normally invisible to

conscious experience.

Broughton (2006) presents

research paper on two stage Psi process.

Presentation of information on other

aspects of Psi process not previously

reported upon. The findings and theories

presented are a good general dissemination

of information. The two stage Psi model

consists of stage one – how ESP 'gets into

the system" – which remains a mystery and

Stage two which is thought to involve the

normal cognitive processes. The research

paper implies that if evolution has conferred

upon humans the ability to make use of

anomalous information then it is likely to

follow the pattern in which existing brain

systems are adapted and enhanced to confer

new advantages. The context of the two-

stage model of receptive psi, would lead one

to expect that evolution would have adapted

existing brain systems to capitalize on

anomalous, psi-based information required

in order to serve survival goals. The

memory systems in the brain have been

identified that mediates anomalous

information into conscious awareness.

However the issue of how the particular

memory images are selected remained

unaddressed and further research needs to be

conducted in this area.

Roe and Holt (2007) conducted a

study using forty participants and generated

virtual readings consisting of twenty-four

statements, eight from each of the three

selection methods used in experiments. This

was a confirmation study of an earlier study

that showed positive results to existence of

psi. Results showed significant interaction

was found between target lability and sender

lability, replicating earlier effect. The study

also showed that any PK sender effect is

sensitive to situational variables and that

these form complex interaction patterns.

Researchers stated that goal and process-

orientation may be confounded by factors

such as activity-passivity that co vary with

this variable.

Brain Wave Patterns

Tucker (2009) summarized research

just being started by David Poeppel and

researchers at The University of California

for the US Army. They received a grant to

study synthetic telepathy. The study is of electrical impulses in the brain and the impulses effect related to telepathy. They plan to relate brain wave electrical impulses to thought patterns. Researches hope to train subjects to think in code patterns like Morse code with the code being picked up by sensors trained to focus on electromagnetic frequency in the brain and then send detection to a computer or resent to another sensor. Their theory is that motor memory gives a big signal and can be read or extracted. All mental thoughts create electrical signals. This would allow something like helmet to helmet telepathic communication as quoted in the article.

Moulton and Kosslyn (2008)
conducted experiments using neuroimaging
(MRI) to monitor brain resonance patterns in
trying to resolve the Psi debate. The
experiments were unique in that they actual
monitored brain wave patterns. The findings
showed no conclusive evidence and may
provide the strongest evidence yet obtained
against the existence of paranormal mental
phenomena. MRI imaging is hard to read
and the Psi influence may be using a
different energy field yet undiscovered that
relates to anomalous characteristics. MRI's
may not accurately pick up the psychic
energy field.

Begley (2008) summarizes research studies providing information that could prove the existence of Psi, Telepathy, and ESP are related to brain electrical energy and can be measured with a mind reading dictionary and development of a mind reading machine made possible. Mind reading technology is advancing quickly. The author states that less than three years ago, it was a big deal when studies measured brain activity in people looking at a grating slanted either left or right; fMRI patterns in the visual cortex revealed which grating the volunteers saw.

UNANIMOUS ANONYMOUS V -TELEPATHY-ESP-
REALITY?

Research has broken the "content"

barrier. Scientists at Carnegie Mellon

University showed people drawings of

five tools (hammer, drill and the like)

and five dwellings (castle, igloo ...) and

asked them to think about each object's

properties, uses and any thing else that

came to mind. Meanwhile, fMRI

measured activity throughout each

volunteer's brain. The activity patterns

evoked by each object were so

distinctive that the computer could tell

with seventy-eight percent accuracy

when someone was thinking about a

hammer and not, say pliers. CMU

neuroscientist Marcel Just thinks they

can improve the accuracy (which

reached ninety-four percent for one

person) if people hold still in the fMRI

and keep their thoughts from drifting to,

say, lunch.

The results have to be

replicated by independent labs

before they can be accepted.

This is the first time any mind-

reading technique has

achieved such specificity.

Remarkably, the activity

patterns -- from visual areas to

movement area to regions that

encode abstract ideas like the

feudal associations of a castle -

- were eerily similar from one

person to another. The report

indicated that there is a

commonality in how different

people's brains represent the

same object.

The report indicated

that the more detailed the

thought is, the more different

these patterns get, because

different people have different

associations for an object or

idea The CMU group is

determining the brain patterns

that encode abstract ideas

(honesty, democracy), words

and sentences, a big step

toward a mind-reading

dictionary The article provides

the most supportive

explanation of the reality of

telepathy and ESP related to

brain electrical patterns.

Sheldrake (2003) wrote an article

explaining his theory on explaining

telepathy and other phenomena. Mental

fields are rooted in the brains energy

fields. The example using magnets can

best explain it. Magnetic fields around

magnets are rooted in the magnets

themselves, or just as the fields of

transmission around mobile phones are

rooted in the phones and their internal electrical activities. As magnetic fields extend around magnets, electromagnetic fields also extend around mobile phones. This analogy can be related to mental fields extending around brains.

Mental fields can be used to help explain telepathy, also the sense of being stared at and other widespread but unex-plained abilities. Above all, mental fields underlie normal perception. They are an essential part of vision. The mind mental energy related to vision may give of an energy field in the brains processing of this information.

Ganzfeld Experiments

UNANIMOUS ANONYMOUS V -TELEPATHY-ESP-REALITY?

Bem, Palmer, and Broughton (2001)

The Ganzfeld database may be a victim of its own success. Ganzfeld experiments have been around for a long time and have become a test standard for ESP testing. Article presents view that the Ganzfeld procedure appears to provide replicable evidence for Psi. The term "psi" denotes anomalous processes of information transfer. Many studies have been conducted and this article lists some of them. The Ganzfeld procedure uses two participants as a sender and as a receiver. It is an established set standard for telepathic studies. The article rated studies that used the Ganzfeld procedure. The researchers suggest that future meta-analyses should

distinguish "standard" replications from

non-standard extensions of the Ganzfeld

procedure test should it become a victim of

its own success.

Roe and Holt (2006) used an

automated Ganzfeld computer system in

their study. Forty trials were conducted.

Twenty three trials involved senders and

seventeen did not involve senders... The

receivers registered a twenty-five percent hit

rate. This study indicated that the sender

serves some active role in the Ganzfeld

experiment ESP sessions. Results varied

from a previous study. Generally studies

look at consistency of results of the various

studies.   Twenty-five percent hit rates of

receivers are exactly what would be

expected by chance. Results were reported

in table form.

Roe, Holt, and Simmonds (2003)

hypothesized three predictions in the study.

They used Ganzfeld GESP protocol .Forty

participants using an automated Ganzfeld

computer system were tested. The trials used

statements and video clips. An attempt was

made to distinguish between senders and

receivers that participated in the study. The

role of sender has been inconsistent in other

studies and the relationship of receiver and

senders not taken into account. This study

used a novel approach for assessing any

sender influence. Co variation of

performance with the receiver and the

sender variables were evaluated. The

receivers had a thirty-five percent hit rate

which was above the mean chance

expectation. The results were listed in table

form.

Conclusions

In the literature review on the theme

"reality of telepathy", twenty pieces of

literature related to the theme were

researched. They consisted of telephone

surveys, videotaped experiments,

experiments on animals, experiments related

to emails, evaluation of emotional effects,

mothers' interactions with children, and

results related to intimate relationships. The

large majority of the literature reviewed

indicated a greater than chance possibility

that telepathy may be involved in the results

documented in the literature. Some literature

indicated the findings were equal to that of

chance; however that literature was in the

minority of reports researched.

The literature review on the theme

"relationship to ESP" looked at four sources

of information regarding this theme. Areas

were on hypnotic effects, detecting unseen

gazes, the mind machine, and manipulated

expectations. Results showed that hypnosis

and manipulated expectations could

influence and enhance the effects in results

searching for evidence of ESP.

Computerized experiments may have fell

short in getting results because tests were

not conducted in a quiet laboratory setting

and it did not involve mental interaction

with other people, but consisted of trying to

guess outcomes.

The theme "Psi Phenomena" had to

do with research conducted on anomalous

information or unexplained phenomena

related to physical or biological

mechanisms. Five sources of information

were reviewed with one survey showing that

the majority of Psychology Professors do

not believe in telepathy or ESP. Professors

in other fields had a high belief rate in its

existence. This survey results may indicate

why one of today's most leading researcher

in the field is in the biology field and not the

psychology field.

This literature review shows some indication

that when you remove human interaction in

the research study the general results are

equal to that of chance.

The literature review has shown that

research on the brain is only now getting

started. This is a new area of study and the

literature review shows research is heading

in that exciting direction. There is a good

chance of success in developing a device

that can read the brains electrical energy

fields and can indicate what that individuals

mind is thinking. A mind-reading dictionary

is being developed that identifies different

thoughts that result in brain wave patterns,

found to be the same between different

individuals. Researchers are also conducting

experiments for the military. Sheldrake, a

leading researcher theorizes that the mind

gives off energy fields that extend around

the brain. This energy field can be picked up

and read by other peoples' minds. Other

research in identifying the characteristics of

this energy field needs to be conducted.

Ganzfeld experiments have become a

standard of test for telepathy and ESP

among Psychologist researchers. The

experiment relates to a standard computer

test that is used for identifying areas of

anomalous interactions. Some experiments

show more than chance findings and others

show equal to chance findings. Taking the

human interaction between individuals out

of the research equation and relying upon a

computer to give and record response may

not be in the right direction to identifying

the true nature of telepathy and ESP.

In conclusion, more research should

be conducted in areas related to the brains

energy fields, efforts to identify this field,

plus the mechanism that the mind uses in

reading the energy waves given off by a

persons' brain need to be conducted. The

over all literature review gives an indication

that the occurrences of telepathy and ESP

may be more than just mere chance. Man is

still in the dark ages related to research and

understanding of this subject. This literature

review compiles and places in one document

an overview on the subject and indicates the

direction that future research may result in

the most success in determining "How real

is telepathy and ESP?"

References

Alexander, C. H., & Broughton, R. S. (2001, D).

Cerebral Hemisphere Dominance and ESP

Performance in the Autoganzfeld. *The

Journal of Parapsychology, 65*(4), 397-416.

Retrieved April 4, 2009, from Doane

College Wilson web Database.

Begley, S. (2008, Jan 21). Mind Reading is Now Possible. *Newsweek, 151*(3), 22.

Bem, D . J., Palmer, J., & Broughton , R . S. (2001, S). Updating the Ganzfeld Database: A Victim of Success. *The Journal of Parapsychology, 65*(3), 207-18. Retrieved April 4, 2009, from Doane College Wilson web Database.

Bem, D. J., & Honorton, C. (n.d.). Does Psi Exist? Replicable Evidence for an Anomalous Process of Information Transfer. *Psychological Bulletin, 115*(1), 4-18. Retrieved April 4, 2009, from Doane College Ebscohost Database.

Broughton, R. S. (2006, Fall). Memory,

Emotion, and the Receptive Psi Process. *The Journal of Parapsychology, 70*(2), 255-74. Retrieved April 4, 2009, from Doane College Wilson web Database.

Brown, D. J., & Sheldrake, R. (2001, Je). The Anticipation of Telephone Calls: A Survey in California. *The Journal of Parapsychology, 65*(2), 145-66. Retrieved April 4, 2009, from Doane College Wilson web Database.

Carpenter, J. C. (2008, Spr/Fall). Relations Between ESP and Memory in Light of the First Sight Model of Psi. *The Journal of Parapsychology, 72*, 47-76. Retrieved April 18, 2009, from Doane College Wilson web Database.

Colwell, J., Schroder, S., & Sladen, D. (2000).

The Ability to Detect Unseen Staring. A

literature Review and Empirical Tests. *The*

British Journal of Psychology, 91(1), 71-85.

Retrieved April 4, 2009, from Doane

College Wilson web Database.

DeGraaf, T. K., & Houtkooper, J. M. (2004,

Spr). Anticipatory Awareness of

Emotionally Charged Targets by Individuals

with Histories of Emotional Trauma. *The*

Journal of Parapsychology, 68(1), 93-127.

Retrieved April 4, 2009, from Doane

College Wilson web Database.

Moss, T., & Gengerelli, J. A. (1967). Telepathy

and Emotional Stimuli. *Journal of Abnormal*

Psychology, 72(4), 341-348. Retrieved April

4, 2009, from Doane College Ebscohost
Database.

Moulton, S. T., & Kosslyn, S. M. (2008). Using
Neuroimaging to Resolve the Psi Debate.
Journal of Cognitive Neuroscience, 20(1),
182-192.

Murray, C. D., Howard, T., Wilde, D., Fox, J., &
Simmonds-Moore, C. (2007, Spr/Fall).
Testing for Telepathy Using an Immersive
Virtual Environment. *The Journal of
Parapsychology, 71*, 105-23. Retrieved
April 4, 2009, from Doane College Wilson
web Database.

Owens, N . E., & Pitman, J. A. (2004, Spr). The
Effect of Manipulating Expectations Both
Before and During a Test of ESP. *The*

Journal of Parapsychology, 68(1), 45-63.

Retrieved April 4, 2009, from Doane

College Wilson web Database.

Polls Show Paranormal Beliefs on the Rise,

Evolution Belief on the Decline. (2001).

Skeptic, 9(1), 10-11. Retrieved April 4,

2*009*, from Doane College Wilson web

Database.

Roe , C. A., Holt, N. J., & Simmonds, C. A.

(2003, Spr). Considering the Sender as a PK

Agent in Ganzfeld ESP Studies. *The Journal

of Parapsychology, 67*(1), 129-45. Retrieved

April 4, 2009, from Doane College Wilson

web Database.

Roe, C. A., & Holt, N. (2006, Spr). A Further

Consideration of the Sender as a PK Agent

in Ganzfeld ESP Studies. *The Journal of Parapsychology, 69*(1), 113-27. Retrieved April 4, 2009, from Doane College Wilson web Database.

Roe, C. A., & Holt, N. J. (2007, Spr). The Effects of Strategy and Feedback on Performance of a PK Task. *The Journal of Parapsychology, 70*(1), 69-90. Retrieved April 4, 2009, from Doane College Wilson web Database.

Sheldrake, R. (2000, July). The Unexplained Power of Animals. *ISAZ Newsletter*

Sheldrake, R. (2003). Mind Fields. *Resurgence - London - Navern Road*

Sheldrake, R. (2005). The Non-Visual Detection of Staring - Response to Commentators.

Journal of Consciousness Studies, 12(6), 117-126.

Sheldrake, R. (2006). Apparent Telepathy Between Babies and Nursing Mothers. *Sheldrake Papers www.sheldrake.org.* Retrieved May 12, 2009, from Google Scholar with keyword telepathy and author Sheldrake Database.

Sheldrake, R., & Morgan, A. (2003). Testing a Language-Using Parrot for Telepathy. *Journal of Scientific Exploration, 17*(4), 601-616.

Sheldrake, R., & Smart, P. (2000). A Dog that seems to know when his Owner is Coming Home. *Journal of Scientific Exploration, 14*(2), 223-255.

Sheldrake, R., & Smart, P. (2003, July).
Experimental Tests for Telephone
Telepathy. *Journal of the Society for
Psychical Research, 67*, 184-199. Retrieved
April 4, 2009, from Doane College
Ebscohost Database.

Sheldrake, R., & Smart, P. (2003, Spr).
Videotaped Experiments on Telephone
Telepathy. *The Journal of Parapsychology,
67*(1), 147-66. Retrieved April 4, 2009, from
Doane College Wilson web Database.

Sheldrake, R., & Smart, P. (2005). Testing for
Telepathy in Connection with E-mails.
Perceptual and Motor Skills, 101, 771-786.

Sheldrake, R., Godwin, H., & Rockell, S.
(2004). A Filmed Experiment on Telephone

Telepathy with the Nolan Sisters. *Journal of the Society for Psychical Research, 68*, 168-172.

Sheldrake, R., Lawlor, C., & Turney , J. (n.d.). Perceptive Pets: A Survey in London. *Sheldrake Web site www.sheldrake.org.*

Smith, J. (2005, S). A New Way of Seeing. *The Ecologist, 35*(7), 52-6. Retrieved April 18, 2009, from Doane College Wilson web Database.

Thomas, G., & Fletcher, G. J. (2003, Dec). Mind-Reading Accuracy in Intimate Relationships. *Journal of Personality and Social Psychology, 85*(6), 1079-1094. Retrieved April 4, 2009, from Doane College Ebscohost Database.

To The Editor. (2003, Fall). *The Journal of Parapsychology, 67*(2), . Retrieved April 4, 2009, from Doane College Wilson web Database.

Tressold, P., & Prete, G. D. (2007, Spr/Fall). ESP under Hypnosis: The Role of Inductions and Personality Characteristics. *The Journal of Parapsychology, 71*, 125-37. Retrieved April 4, 2009, from Doane College Wilson web Datab

Tucker, P. (2009, Ja/F). David Poeppel, Master of Synthetic Telepathy. *The Futurist, 43*(1), 23. Retrieved April 4, 2009, from Doane College Wilson web Database.

Vassy, Z. (2004, Fall). A Study of Telepathy by Classical Conditioning. *The Journal of*

Parapsychology, 68(2), 323-50. Retrieved

April 4, 2009, from Doane College Wilson

web Database.

Wassner, S. (2005, Mr). Are Twins Mind

Readers. *National Geographic Kids*, (348)

pp. 32-3. Retrieved April 18, 2009, from

Doane College Wilson web Database.

Wiseman, R., & Greening, E. (2002, N). The

Mind Machine: A Mass Participation

Experiment into the Possible Existence of

Extra-sensory Perception. *The British

Journal of Psychology, 93*(3), 487-99.

Retrieved April 4, 2009, from Doane

College Wilson web Database.

www.ingramcontent.com/pod-product-compliance
Lightning Source LLC
Chambersburg PA
CBHW060755260726
48660CB00002B/626